Getting Rid of Resentments

Greg G.

Getting Rid of Resentments

HAZELDEN

Hazelden
Center City, Minnesota 55012-0176

About the pamphlet
If you examine almost any problem that comes between people, you
will probably find resentment, or old anger, lurking near the heart of
the matter. You can dredge up hurt and anger over and over, or you
can let go of resentments and get on with healthy living. Using the
guidance in this pamphlet as a road map, you can steer a course to
freedom from your resentments.

About the author
Greg G. has served as a Lutheran pastor in a small town in Nebraska
and has also been a family counselor. He is currently a chaplain at a
chemical dependency treatment center in Minnesota. He and his wife
have two sons.

Introduction: the tale of the monks

Once upon a time, two Japanese monks were walking along a road together. The rain the evening before had left large puddles in their path, so they made their way with care. When they came upon an intersection covered by an especially large puddle of mud, they noticed a young woman who had stopped at the edge of the puddle. She was dressed in a white silk kimono, and her dilemma was obvious: there was no way she could cross the intersection without soiling her gown.

The first of the two monks asked the woman if she would like some help. She answered yes. The monk then scooped her up in his arms, walked straight through the mud, and put her down on the other side. The woman thanked him and continued on her way.

The monks resumed their journey, but a rift had developed between them. The second monk refused to speak to the first. They walked together in an uneasy silence until that evening when they reached their destination, the lodging temple. It was there that the second monk turned to the first, pointed his finger, and demanded, "Why did you do it?"

The first monk was taken by surprise. "Do what?" he asked.

"Don't play dumb with me!" snapped the second monk. "You know what I'm talking about. You know very well we monks are not supposed to have anything to do with women, especially shapely young women such as the one you carried across the puddle back at the intersection. Tell me, why did you do it? Why did you pick her up?"

The first monk paused for a moment, shrugged, and then replied, "I put her down a long time ago. Maybe you're the one still carrying her."

The story raises what may seem an obvious question: What (or whom) are you still carrying after all these miles?

It is the question of resentment.

The Big Book of Alcoholics Anonymous calls resentments "the number-one offender." Resentment is the greatest enemy chemically dependent people face and the biggest contributor to relapse. In fact, resentments pose a considerable problem for many people, not just those who are chemically dependent. If you examine almost any problem that comes between people, you will probably find a resentment lurking near the heart of the matter. Resentment is a common human problem—and often a severe one.

The word *resent* means to "re-sense" or "re-feel." It is one thing to feel a feeling, such as anger. It is another thing to replay a scene or a conversation in your mind, dredging up the hurt and the anger again and again.

Certainly anger has its place in the emotional makeup of a healthy human being. Anger can be an honest and appropriate response in certain situations. But there is nothing good to be said for "old anger," or resentment. Resentment has no positive side; it is simply a destructive emotion.

What is a resentment?

Have you ever thought of resentment in terms of a drug? Dwelling on your resentment can simulate a "high" of sorts. You might recall what someone said or did to you in the past, and it was not fair! The recollection of that

2

scene can offer a certain rush. Recalling past injustices can make you "feel good."

Carrying a resentment is also a way in which people can justify their actions. It is a way people vindicate themselves in their own minds and boost their self-esteem. Resentful people like to think of themselves as "in the right." By training their attention on the wrong someone has done, they can get the voice in the back of their minds to whisper, *I would never do anything like that.* By holding someone else beneath the weight of their judgment, they place themselves on a self-made pedestal. By focusing their attention on someone else's faults (real or imagined), they keep the focus off their own shortcomings.

When we are resentful we are reluctant to let go of hurt or anger. Resentment is our unwillingness to accept someone who has harmed us or some system or institution that has treated us unjustly. Our fight against acceptance is at the core of our resentments. Our refusal to accept people for who they are, just as they are, our refusal to leave the past alone—these things keep our resentments alive, and continually threaten our serenity.

What is more, we victimize ourselves by our resentments. From somewhere comes the notion that we are in control when we hang on to resentments. We think that hanging on to the pain of the past will keep us from being hurt in the future.

But we are not in control. Indeed, clinging to resentment is a mark of being out of control. We fret about past injustices, real or imagined. We hold on to a resentment against someone who might have no recollection of an offense against us. This can leave us in a very painful spot—alone with our resentments.

Despite its obvious dangers, resentment can become a comfortable routine, a familiar rut we can return to again and again. This rut can become a spiritual problem for recovering people, for resentments cut us off from our Higher Power, families, friends, or co-workers. In fact, resentments cut us off from enjoying life. But most importantly, resentments are the number-one threat to serenity or sobriety. We can choose to keep them, but the price is high. They are, as the Big Book says, luxuries we cannot afford.

How resentments affect me personally

If we want to live with serenity, if we are chemically dependent but desire to have sobriety, then resentment is a sort of pampering we cannot afford. Here is how I began to see resentment for what it is.

My father's storehouse of anger

Some years ago my father was treated for his alcoholism. While he was at the treatment center my mother told him, "I will not live with your anger anymore. You need to find a different way to deal with your anger in the treatment center. Do not bring yourself home from treatment angry. That will not go with me anymore."

My mother was not talking about my father's ordinary frustrations or his irritability when things did not seem to go his way. She was referring to his resentments, his storehouse of anger.

When I think back to my childhood, I remember my father as an angry man. He had a temper like an active volcano, ever ready to blow. He would not, or could not, let go of old hurts. He was not able to cancel old grievances. It did not matter whether his resentments were two days old, two years old, or twenty years old. He cherished them. They fueled his anger.

Whether someone had offended my father, or whether he imagined as much (there is really no difference between the two), he held his resentments tightly. Over the years he became a shriveled and dangerous man. His resentments ate at his insides. Ultimately he drove his family away, along with any friends he had, all because he could not let go of his resentments.

My face-to-face encounter with old anger
Some time ago I took my own Fourth and Fifth Steps, as suggested in the Big Book of Alcoholics Anonymous. (In the Fourth Step you make a list of your defects of character, and of your positive qualities. In the Fifth Step you share the list with another person, trusting that a Higher Power is present when you do so.) When I took these Steps I had to claim some of my own resentments; I had no idea that there were so many of them or that they ran so deep. I had once thought that resentment was my father's problem, and his undoing, but my Fourth Step brought me face-to-face with my own old anger. I, too, had a deep capacity to be hurt and to stay hurt.

It occurred to me that I had been spending a great deal of time pampering myself with my resentments. I recognized that it was simply time to "set the lady down." I needed to let go of some things and accept some of the pain that was part of my personal history.

If you grew up in a home beset by alcoholism or some similar trauma, the day may come when you will need to learn how to deal with your resentments in a constructive way. You may need to break away from the methods you learned in your family of origin. You will need to discover ways to let go of the anger that is holding back your recovery. In the following section I shall present some healthy ways to address the problem of resentment.

Letting go

How do you let go of resentments? of hurt? of anger? It is not easy. If we were to take a poll, we might find that many people want to let go of their resentments, but do not know how to get started.

How do you let go of resentments? Perhaps the best way to respond to this question is with another question: How do you open your fist? My fist opens when I become willing for it to do so. I do not need to do a lot of thinking about *how* to unclench my fist. My willingness is what opens it.

It is the same with resentments. It is not as important to pursue the question of *how* to let go of resentments as it is to become willing to relax your grip.

Though there is no magic formula that guarantees your resentments will be whisked away, I can offer four questions that might help you. These four questions are paraphrased from chapter 5 of the Big Book:

1. With whom am I angry?
Where is my anger directed? How is it blocking my peace of mind? Some people might be able to fire off a list of people or institutions with which they are angry or frustrated. It would be most helpful, however, to start with just one person or institution. If you are angry with a long list of people or institutions, who or what would be at the top of that list? If you could let go of your resentment for that one person or situation, it would be a good day's work. Once you have decided to let go of this resentment, discuss it with someone at a Twelve Step meeting, or with a sponsor, counselor, or friend.

2. How have I been hurt?
In what way have I been injured? What part of me has been harmed enough for me to cling to my resentment?

Has someone damaged my pride? my reputation? my sense of trust? my sexual boundaries?

Resentment is like a coin, with the face of anger on one side and hurt on the other. Some folks are obviously angry people. You can spot them across a room, and you might tend to give them a wide berth. Angry people continually fume about the injustices they have experienced. They need little encouragement to rehash their grievances and vent their hostility.

When you turn over the coin of resentment you find that these angry people have been hurt deeply. That hurt lies just beneath their angry exterior. Instead of going on and on about how angry they are, these people need to look upon themselves as needing healing and care.

Then there are people who wear their hurt on their sleeve. They may have sadness and tears about some relationship in their lives, but they cannot bring themselves to blame that person or to be angry. "I could *never* be angry with her after all she has done for me," they explain plaintively. "After all, she is my daughter!"

When these people become ready to get rid of their resentment, they may unearth anger that has been buried for years. While digging around, they may even discover the conviction that they deserve to be treated with respect.

3. Am I able to look upon the other person differently?
Can I find compassion for the person who has hurt me? Can I understand what motivated the person to do what he or she did? Can I suspend my pain long enough to try to comprehend—not to justify what the person has done, but to understand—what might dispose a person to behave toward me in such a fashion? Can I think of something in this person's past or present situation that might cause him or her to lash out at me?

These are yes or no questions, of course. If my answers to these questions are yes, I have found compassion in my heart. If my answers are no—if I am not able to look upon the other person differently—then I get to keep my resentments. I am stuck with them.

Letting go of my resentment requires that I soften or change my attitude toward the person who has brought harm to me. The other person might apologize, make amends to me, or even perform backflips, but I shall not be done with my resentment until I decide I am ready. Make no mistake about it: I am responsible for dealing with my own feelings of resentment. Only I can get rid of them, and this only when I am prepared to look at the other person in a different light.

4. What is my part of the problem?

When I feel resentful I often focus on the wrong someone else has done. In so doing I get hung up. I am a prisoner of my own perspective when the only fault I can see is someone else's.

In the first place, I cannot undo the harm someone has done to me. No one can. If it happened, it happened. In the second place, I cannot make someone treat me differently. I might tell the person how I would like to be treated, but I have no guarantee that the harm will not be repeated. In other words, as long as I train my attention toward the wrong that someone else has brought about, I have nothing in my hands. I have no control over my resentment; I have nothing with which I can work. I have given my power and my control to the other person.

When I am ready to take responsibility for my own feelings, when I am prepared to take charge of my resentment, I begin by asking myself about my contribution to the problem. Even if someone else was primarily to blame—even 95 percent at fault—I ask myself about my 5 percent. What did I contribute, even if it was minimal? What can I do differently in future relationships? It requires a good measure of humility to train your attention on your own part of the problem—especially when someone else clearly has been in the wrong—but it can help you gain control of your resentment.

There may be situations in which someone else was completely at fault. Perhaps I had no part in the problem whatsoever. I simply walked into a room, for example, and bore the brunt of someone else's rage. In such an instance, when I was not at fault in the least, my part of the problem might be that I have clung to my resentment against that person for two days, or two weeks, or two months, or two years. My part of the problem might be my tendency for keeping, or even cherishing, old anger or old hurt. When I become ready to take responsibility for my resentment, I begin by looking at my own part of the problem.

Keeping my own side of the street clean is enough

I was raised in a home where alcoholism was present. Naturally I collected a long list of grievances against my alcoholic father for the way he treated me and the rest of the family. I grew up with those resentments clutched in my fists. I remember a time in college when I was sitting at a library desk and supposedly working on a research paper, but my mind was replaying scenes of havoc from my childhood. I was aware of how angry I was by how hard I gripped my pencil.

But that was then and this is now. My father (and his disease) had created considerable hurt in my family, but I found that I was the one who kept re-creating the incidents in my mind. At one time my father and his disease had been responsible for the pain, but now I was responsible for giving life to those scenes, and the pain, all over again.

After I had been involved with Al-Anon for some years, I took a look at those still-clenched fists of mine. It occurred to me that I had a firm grip on the faults and frailties of my father. I asked myself—and this did not come naturally to me—what harm I had brought him. When had I interfered with his life or his happiness? Although I had a long list of grievances against my father at the ready—I had been rehearsing them for years—I could think of only a few instances in which I regretted my words or my behavior toward him, such as my strong sarcasm when he finally entered a treatment program for his alcoholism. (This was in the days before I understood that chemical dependency is a disease.)

When I finally unclenched my fists I wrote a letter to my father, seeking to make amends for the pain I added to his life. It does not make very much sense to apologize to someone who has hurt you, but in my case, it helped put the focus on myself rather than on my father. It helped me to relax my fists. What my father and his disease had done to me and my family *did* happen, but they were no longer my responsibility. I was no longer "the sheriff," duty-bound to bring my father face-to-face with my interpretation of justice. Keeping my own side of the street clean would be enough.

More suggestions for dealing with resentments

Here are some suggestions about how you might deal with resentments in your life. I offer no 100 percent guarantees. These suggestions, however, have been very helpful for me and may also be useful for you. Focus on what you believe is best in your situation.

Write or talk about it

In the tradition of Alcoholics Anonymous and Al-Anon, the best way to let go of resentments involves a Fourth and Fifth Step—writing down your resentments, then sharing your list with someone you trust. Instead of keeping your resentments to yourself or complaining about your ill will toward others, you might deal more constructively with your resentments by committing them to writing. Your resentments might seem a lot different on paper than they do rattling around in your mind.

If you are willing to share your list of resentments with another person, you might find that the resentments are only half as weighty as you once thought. Though you may never forget completely the harm someone has caused you, the whole thing may not seem so charged with painful emotions anymore.

ஃ

Can you share your resentments with
another person whom you trust?

Discipline yourself

Can I discipline myself not to react rashly to the unkind words and deeds of others? Can I train myself not to dwell on the anger and hurt from my past? Can I catch myself when I begin to dredge up my resentments? Can I develop the presence of mind to tell myself, *It is a Sunday afternoon, the sun is shining, and there is nothing for me to gain by replaying a scene that took place six months ago?*

I once knew a fellow who wanted to condition himself against his resentments. He wore a blue rubber band on his left wrist, and a red one on his right. The blue band represented self-pity, the red one resentment. Whenever he would start feeling sorry for himself, he would give the blue band a snap. When he would catch himself feeling resentful, he would snap the red one. Sometimes his wife would help him too. On occasion, when he had said something that sounded resentful, she would reach across the dining room table and pluck at the red rubber band. It was a silly gimmick, to be sure. Can you think of a better method?

❧

Can you discipline yourself not to stew
in resentments, or are you a slave to your
destructive feelings?

Pray

Have you ever tried praying for someone you resent? Have you considered praying for someone *precisely because* that person has harmed you? It is not logical to pray for someone who has done you wrong, but would it help you deal with your resentful attitude toward that person? You might begin by praying, "God bless and keep this person . . . far away from me." The Big Book suggests that you think first of the things you would ask for yourself in prayer—health, happiness, or friendship—and then pray that the person you resent might have these same things.

I knew a woman who possessed great bitterness toward her alcoholic father for the pain he had caused her during her childhood. In an effort to let go of her resentment, she resolved that she would pray for him every night for two weeks. Although she started out praying for him with clenched teeth, she found that after two weeks she could pray naturally and without anger. She made progress.

❧

Would it be helpful to pray for someone
you resent? Can you do this precisely because
that person has harmed you?

Perform an act of kindness

Have you ever thought of doing or saying something kind to someone who has hurt you—perhaps even *because* the person has hurt you? It does not make sense to repay unkindness with kindness; it is more natural to repay hurt with more hurt or resentment. But would making some kind of a generous gesture help you rise above your resentment? Would it help you treat the other person as you would like to be treated?

Some years ago I accepted a position as a pastor in a small town in Nebraska. When I pulled into town, little did I realize that I was stepping into a boiling pot of church politics. At my very first church council meeting, I became aware of a heated issue surrounding the propriety of having military funerals in the church. Some council members believed a church building was the wrong place for rifles, marching men in uniforms, and a flag draped over a casket. Other council members, especially the veterans, insisted that these things were perfectly appropriate.

I was in the middle of a conflict I did not want. When I tried to be diplomatic and give equal weight to both sides of the dispute, one of the veterans got angry with me, presumably because I did not side with him from the beginning. He treated me with sarcasm and contempt.

His spiteful words triggered my resentment. For months thereafter I tasted and retasted his bitter words. In those days I made regular trips to a hospital, about an hour's drive away, to visit parishioners. During that drive I would think back on how that man had beaten me up with his words, and I would become enraged. I would argue with the man. I would shout at him as I drove along in my car. I would relive the whole scene over and over again and would work myself into a frenzy.

When I reached the hospital, I quickly shifted gears,

put on my best pastoral demeanor, and acted sane as I made my calls. Once I returned to my car, however, my fiendish feelings would reemerge, and I would bellow at the man all the way home. For all I knew, the guy was sitting in the local cafe, drinking coffee with the boys, and enjoying his afternoon. But I was busy seething over the incident, shrieking at him from behind my steering wheel.

After one of these trips my wife asked what was the matter with my voice. She said I sounded hoarse. The matter with me was that I had a tremendous resentment, or rather, it had me. I needed to find a way to let go of my hatred.

Shortly before Christmas, I went to the grocery store and purchased a box of apples. I wrapped the box in Christmas paper and took it to church with me on Christmas morning. After the worship service I stood by the door, shaking hands with parishioners. All the while the box was under my arm. When the fellow who had once insulted me filed past, I bade him "Merry Christmas," shook his hand, and presented the gift to him. (No, there were no worms or any other foreign objects in the apples.)

I suppose I gave the box of apples to the man because I hated him for what he had done to me. He stammered a word of thanks, and was gone. It does not make much sense for a person to give a gift to someone he despises, but in my case it helped me let go of my attitude of resentment. I was able to treat him more graciously than he had treated me, and that felt good to me.

Today I do not count this man as one of my close friends. We do not exchange Christmas cards. I can honestly say, however, that I do not resent him anymore. I do not even think of him very often. When I do, I do not replay old feelings of anger.

❧

Have you considered speaking a friendly word to
or doing a kind deed for someone you resent,
precisely because that person has hurt you?

Be assertive

I once knew a businesswoman who was very sensitive.
She had a hard time accepting criticism from other people, and she knew it. She frequently attended meetings in
the course of her work and often felt offended by things
said to her or about her when her associates were gath-
ered. She knew she was too easily "bruised," but did not
know what to do about her foible. She had a problem
with resentment.

In order to keep from taking on resentments so easily,
she decided she needed to become more assertive. Whenever anyone said anything that gave rise to her defensive-
ness, she made it a point to ask the person afterward in
private, "Did you mean to offend me by what you said?"
or "Were you trying to hurt my feelings when you made
that comment?"

If the other person replied, "Well, no, I did not mean to
attack you personally," then she told herself she would
take that person at his or her word. She resolved that she
would believe that person had not sought to insult her.
She told herself she did not need to feel offended because
the other person had no intention of hurting her. She han-
dled her problem with resentments by asserting herself.
Her story suggests that we do not have to get angry if we
are willing to be assertive in the first place.

❧

Might assertiveness be an alternative
to taking on new resentments?

15

Accept the painful experience

When you are thinking about ways to deal with resentment, perhaps acceptance is the best way of all. Maybe the issue of resolving old anger boils down to this: where I have resentment in my life, there is something I have not accepted yet. A solution to the problem of resentment is simple acceptance. According to the Serenity Prayer, we accept the things we cannot change. It says nothing about harboring a grudge.

If someone has said something about me that is either untrue or unkind, maybe I need to accept that this is the way the other person sees me. That person may have a twisted perspective, but I can accept it as his or her way of viewing me. There is an adage that goes something to the effect of, "What you think of me is none of my business," a statement of acceptance if there ever was one.

When I remember an especially painful experience in my childhood, for example, maybe I need to accept that this is indeed a part of my personal history. Instead of protesting that something was not fair, I might accept that it did happen to me, and then get on with the rest of my life. The alternative to accepting my past would be to indulge in resentment or, in other words, to keep reliving that painful past.

&

Where you have resentment, what is it
that you are refusing to accept?

Do not respond to the ridiculous

If someone has said something to me or about me that is clearly exaggerated or absurd, I can choose to let it go, rather than taking offense at the remark. When I react to a statement that is obviously unreasonable or spiteful, I am granting a measure of respectability to it. One man

16

put it simply: "If you resent what someone has said about you, at some level you must agree with the person." When we take someone's caustic words seriously, we give away our own serenity, or power, too readily.

Blaming, sarcasm, and ridicule—which often are present in relationships where chemical dependency is a factor—frequently lead to arguments. When people argue they cease to communicate. One good way to curb verbal warfare, and to avoid resentments, is not to respond to verbal abuse at all. If you find yourself in a relationship with someone who likes to quarrel—someone who likes to make you feel as miserable as he or she already does—it might be best not to react. It might be wise to refuse the bait.

❧

> If you are troubled by the words someone once
> spoke to you, ask yourself these questions: Was
> the statement inaccurate? Was it silly? Was it
> outrageous? Was it downright ridiculous? If it
> was, be done with it. Let it go now.

Let it be

When you have made every effort to deal with a resentment, and it still bothers you, maybe the only answer is to let it be—that is, leave it alone, or let it sleep, at least for today.

I remember a man who was married to an alcoholic. His wife had numerous affairs with other men during her drinking days. Although she was now in recovery and was no longer having affairs, resentment still smoldered within this man. He had asked her dozens of times to explain why she had been unfaithful to him, but he had never felt satisfied with her account. He knew he should forgive his wife, but he was not able to do so. He even felt

17

in his heart that he wanted to forgive her, but he could not manage it.

This same man went to some Al-Anon meetings and talked about the difficulty he had forgiving his wife. In time, he came to the conclusion that while he was not able to forgive his wife for what she had done, he could *let it be.* He could quit stirring up the painful past; he could quit bringing up the subject with his wife; he could stop throwing the matter back in her face; he could cease asking her to explain herself just one more time. He resolved that if he needed to talk about his feelings regarding this touchy subject, he would speak with someone other than his wife.

If you cannot forgive some harm done to you, perhaps the next best thing is to let it be. The idea of forgiveness is actually not a central concept in Alcoholics Anonymous and Al-Anon. Although you will find the word *forgiveness* used in the literature of these two groups, it is not a key to the program. The notion of forgiveness probably comes more from the influence of Christianity or Judaism. Perhaps letting it be is a good half-step toward forgiveness.

એ

In situations in which you are unable
to forgive, can you just let it be?

Conclusion: the tale of the monkeys

The story is told of an African people who regarded monkey meat as a delicacy especially suited for their festival meals. The monkeys, however, were difficult to capture. They rarely strayed far from the safety of the trees. Whenever the villagers would send in their dogs, the monkeys would scamper into the trees. They were a nimble lot. They would climb too quickly and too high to be knocked down with stones or sticks.

18

Nevertheless, the villagers found a way to get their hands on the monkeys. The people went down to the riverbank to get some clay. With this clay they fashioned crude bottles that were rounded at the bottom and curved up into long, narrow necks. Once the clay hardened, the villagers filled the bottom of these bottles with peanuts and set them out on the floor of the jungle. Then the villagers went home to bed.

During the night, the monkeys smelled the peanuts, sensed that everything was safe, and came swinging down from the trees to investigate. One by one, the monkeys reached down into bottles and grabbed fistfuls of the peanuts. When a monkey tried to retrieve its prize, however, it found it could not pull its fist out of the bottle. Though it strained with all its might, it could not pull the peanuts from the bottle.

The next morning, the people arose and walked out to the clearing in the jungle, where they found the monkeys still trying to jerk their treasures from the bottles. Casually, the villagers scooped up the monkeys, broke the bottles, and carried the animals home to provide stew meat for their festival.

Ultimately the monkeys lost their freedom because they were not willing to let go. They refused to unclench their fists. So it is with our resentments. If we want to be set free from our resentments, most likely we will need to let go of something.

If I want to be released from my old anger or hurt, I shall need to relax my fist. In the end, resentment's grip on me comes down to my grip on it.

When resentment gets you down, remember the monk who could not lay down his load of resentment. Remember, too, the monkeys that would not open their fists. Let go and let God.

Bibliography

Alcoholics Anonymous, 3d ed. New York: Alcoholics Anonymous World Services, Inc., 1976.

Bausch, William J. *Storytelling, Imagination and Faith.* Mystic, Conn.: Twenty-Third Publications, 1984.

Dollard, Jerry. *Toward Spirituality: The Inner Journey.* Center City, Minn.: Hazelden Foundation, 1983.

One Day at a Time in Al-Anon. New York: Al-Anon Family Group Headquarters, Inc., 1973.